BAD BUNNY

Making a Difference as a Rapper

By Therese M. Shea

KidHaven PUBLISHING

People Who Make a Difference

Published in 2027 by
KidHaven Publishing, an Imprint of Greenhaven Publishing, LLC
2544 Clinton St.
Buffalo, NY 14224

Designer: Deanna Lepovich
Editor: Therese Shea

Photo credits: Cover Sipa USA/Alamy Photos; pp. 5, 19, 21 UPI/Alamy Photos; pp. 7, 15, 17 ZUMA Press, Inc./Alamy Photos; p. 7 (inset) Serban Bogdan/Shutterstock.com; p. 9 Stefan Crämer/Alamy Photos; p. 11 Gabriela V. Berg/Shutterstock.com; p. 13 Everett Collection Inc/Alamy Photos; p. 21 (background) T.Sumaetho/Shutterstock.com.

Cataloging-in-Publication Data

Names: Shea, Therese.
Title: Bad Bunny: making a difference as a rapper / Therese M. Shea.
Description: Buffalo, NY : KidHaven Publishing, 2027. | Series: People who make a difference | Includes glossary and index.
Identifiers: ISBN 9781534571556 (pbk.) | ISBN 9781534571563 (library bound) | ISBN 9781534571570 (ebook)
Subjects: LCSH: Bad Bunny, 1994–Juvenile literature. | Singers–Puerto Rico–Biography–Juvenile literature. | Rap musicians–Puerto Rico–Biography–Juvenile literature.
Classification: LCC ML3930.B204 S525 2027 | DDC 782.42164092 B–dc23

Printed in the United States of America

Some of the images in this book illustrate individuals who are models. The depictions do not imply actual situations or events.

CPSIA compliance information: Batch #CSKH27: For further information contact Greenhaven Publishing LLC at 1-844-317-7404.

CONTENTS

THE BIGGEST STAGE

On February 8, 2026, music superstar Bad Bunny stepped in front of his biggest crowd yet. He was the main act for the halftime show of Super Bowl LX (60). He wanted the show to feel like a **Latino** party—and it did. Even people who didn't understand his Spanish music were dancing.

Bad Bunny's halftime show honored Latino **culture**, especially his home of Puerto Rico. Bad Bunny makes a difference by shining a spotlight proudly on Puerto Rico and Latino culture.

In His Words

"I really want people to have fun. It's gonna be a huge party. I want to bring what people can always expect from me, and a lot of my culture."

— Statement at a press conference before Super Bowl LX

Bad Bunny's 2026 Super Bowl halftime show had more than 4 billion online views within 24 hours—the most ever for a halftime show.

YOUNG BENITO

Bad Bunny was born Benito Antonio Martínez Ocasio on March 10, 1994, in Bayamón, Puerto Rico. He was raised in Vega Baja near San Juan, Puerto Rico. His father was a truck driver, and his mother was a teacher. He has two younger brothers: Bernie and Bysael.

Bad Bunny's family listened to many genres, or kinds, of music, including salsa and pop. He sang for his church. As he grew older, he listened to reggaeton, which is a mix of rap and reggae, a kind of Caribbean music. In 2012, he began studying at the University of Puerto Rico.

In His Words

"Responsibility, punctuality [being on time], I learned that from my mom…I remember my dad was always giving and helping like the people from the neighborhood and that part of me…I learned from my dad."

— Interview with Apple Music from January 2025

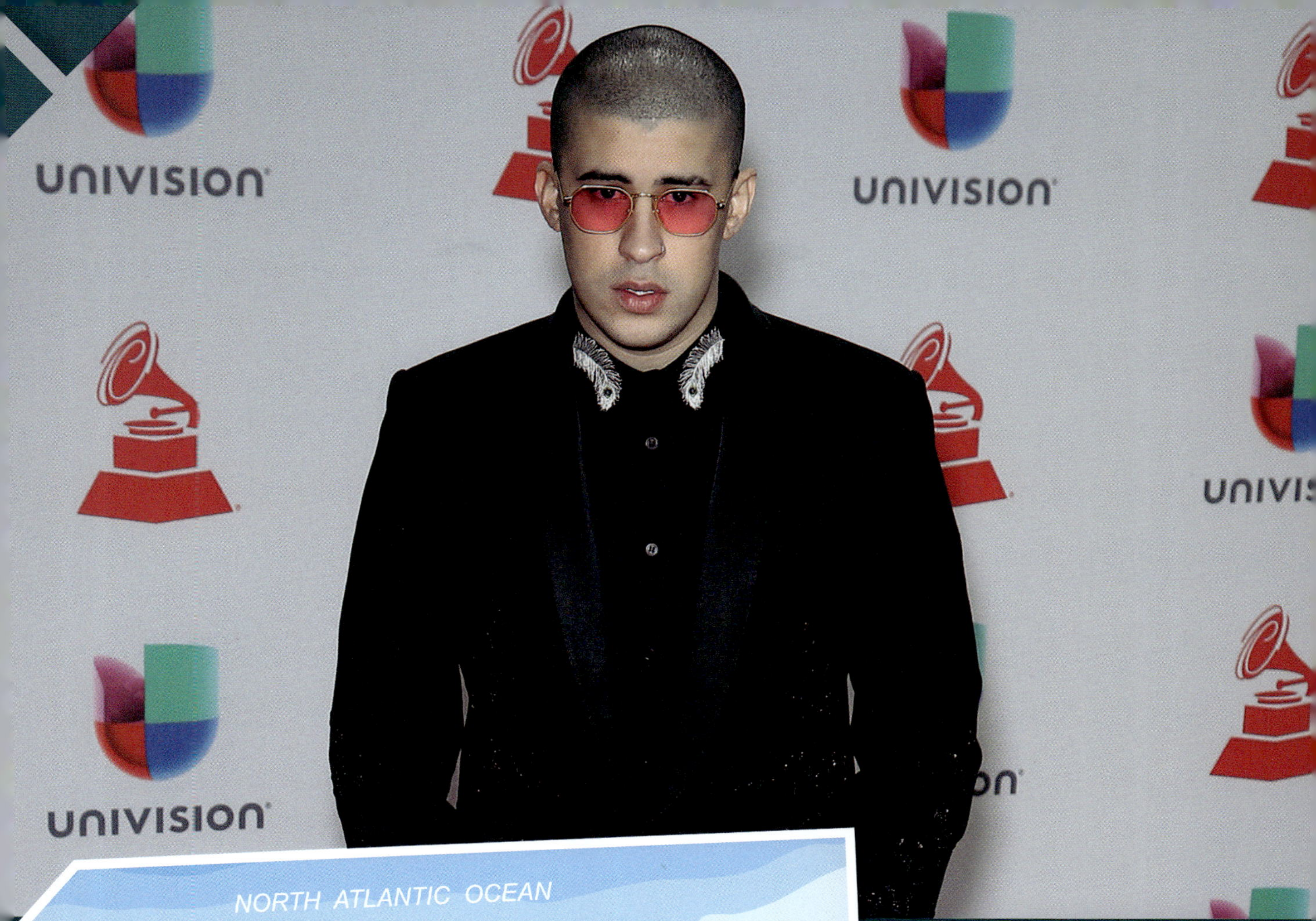

Benito took the name "Bad Bunny" from a childhood photo of himself looking mad in a bunny costume.

EARLY HITS

While he studied, Bad Bunny had a job at a grocery store and worked on his own music. He put his music online. One of his songs, "Diles," got the attention of people in the music business in 2016. He then left school to focus on music.

In 2017, his song with Colombian singer Karol G, "Ahora Me Llama," reached number 10 on the *Billboard* Hot Latin Songs chart. The next year, his song with Cardi B and J Balvin, "I Like It," reached number one on the *Billboard* Hot 100 chart.

In His Words

"I never, ever stopped believing in myself. You should also believe in yourself. You're worth more than you think. Trust me."

— translated from his Super Bowl LX performance on February 8, 2026

In the beginning of his career, Bad Bunny released, or put out, songs and videos on YouTube to gain fans.

FIRST ALBUMS

In 2018, Bad Bunny released his first album, *X 100pre.* Most of its songs were reggaeton and Latin trap, which is a kind of hip-hop music. He went on tour in 2019.

In summer 2019, **protests** began in Puerto Rico. They were partly about a group chat in which the governor took part. Messages on it were disrespectful to women and to **LGBTQ+** people. Other messages joked about deaths caused by Hurricane Maria, which caused terrible harm to Puerto Rico in 2017. Bad Bunny left his tour to join the protests. Finally, the governor stepped down.

In His Words

"I live in Puerto Rico, my family lives in Puerto Rico, my friends. What happens in Puerto Rico matters to me."

— Instagram post from July 2019

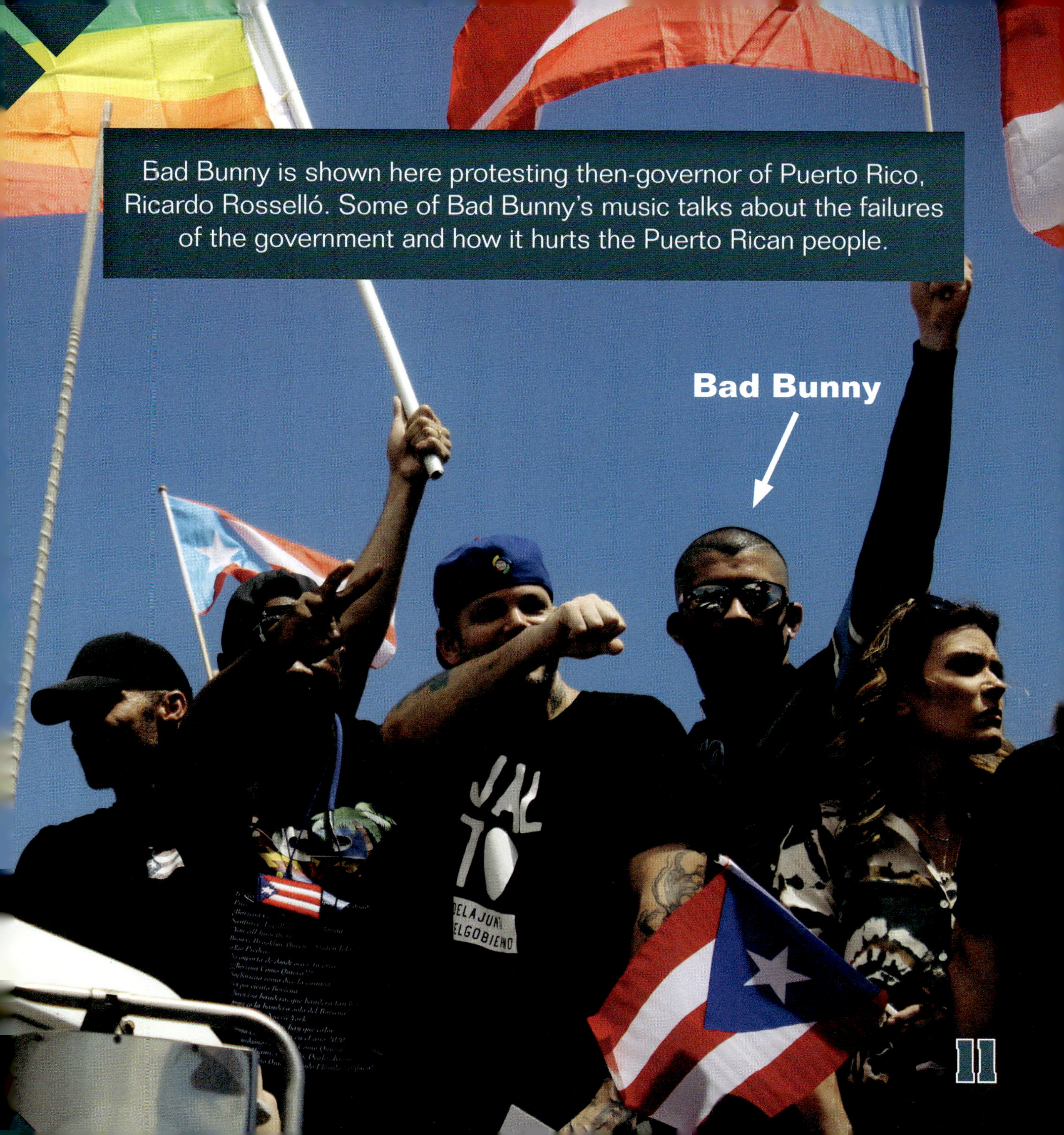

Bad Bunny is shown here protesting then-governor of Puerto Rico, Ricardo Rosselló. Some of Bad Bunny's music talks about the failures of the government and how it hurts the Puerto Rican people.

IN 2020

In 2020, Bad Bunny performed at the Super Bowl halftime show with Shakira and Jennifer Lopez. His reggaeton album *YHLQMDLG* came out in February. The letters stand for *Yo Hago Lo Que Me Da La Gana* (*I Do Whatever I Want*). It debuted, or started, at number 2 on the *Billboard* 200. Soon after, the **COVID-19 pandemic** began.

During the pandemic, Bad Bunny wrote songs while staying in Puerto Rico. He kept in touch with fans through social media. In November, he released the album *El Último Tour del Mundo* (*The Final World Tour*).

In His Words

"I want to **dedicate** this prize to women around the world, especially Latinx and Puerto Rican women...Stop **violence** against women. Let's educate right now, in the present, to have a better future."

— Speech at the Billboard Music Awards on October 14, 2020

In October 2020, Bad Bunny was named Top Latin Artist at the Billboard Music Awards. He spoke against violence toward women during his award speech.

STREAMING SUPERSTAR

Bad Bunny is also interested in music beyond trap and reggaeton. His fourth album, *Un Verano Sin Ti* (*A Summer Without You*), features *cumbia*, a kind of Colombian dance music. His 2023 album *Nadie Sabe Lo Que Va a Pasar Mañana* (*Nobody Knows What Will Happen Tomorrow*) features electronic music.

His sixth album, 2025's *DeBÍ TiRAR MáS FOToS* (*I Should Have Taken More Photos*), included older kinds of Latin music. "I always believed in Latin music, not only in my genre, but in all of them," he said. He wanted younger people to value them too.

In His Words

"Each album that I've made has its own identity [style]."

— Interview with the Associated Press (AP) on November 27, 2020

Bad Bunny is called the "King of Latin Trap," yet he includes many styles in his successful music. He was the most-**streamed** artist in 2020, 2021, 2022, and 2025.

A LOVE FOR HIS LANGUAGE

Bad Bunny sings and performs almost entirely in Spanish. Some have suggested that he sing in English to gain more fans in the United States and other places. He explained that as a Spanish-speaking Puerto Rican, he thinks of his songs in Spanish. He says he's most genuine, or truly himself, when using Spanish.

He also pointed out that his success in the United States and around the world proves that Spanish music can be as popular as English music. He's proud he hasn't changed.

In His Words

"It makes me really proud to get to this level by speaking in Spanish, and not only in Spanish, in the Spanish we speak in Puerto Rico."

— Interview with *El Pais* from January 2021

Although Puerto Rico is a U.S. territory, Spanish is the most-spoken language there.

HIS RECORDS AND FIRSTS

Bad Bunny's music has broken **barriers** in many ways. In 2020, he broke the record for most weeks at number one on the *Billboard* Top Latin Albums chart, for *X 100pre*. That year, *El Último Tour del Mundo* was the first wholly Spanish-language album to reach number one on the *Billboard* 200 chart.

In 2022, *Un Verano Sin Ti* was the first Spanish-language album to be **nominated** for Album of the Year at the Grammy Awards. And in 2026, *DeBÍ TiRAR MáS FOToS* was the first Spanish-language album to win the Grammy for Album of the Year.

In His Words

"I have the power to break **stereotypes** and whatever useless rules that society puts on us."

— Interview with *Rolling Stone* from December 27, 2018

The Life of Bad Bunny

1994
Benito Antonio Martínez Ocasio is born on March 10.

2012
Benito finishes high school and starts at the University of Puerto Rico.

2016
His first hit song, "Diles," is released online.

2018
Bad Bunny's first album, *X 100pre*, is released. It wins a Latin Grammy for Best Urban Music Album.

2019
Bad Bunny leaves his tour to protest the Puerto Rican government.

2020
Bad Bunny releases *El Último Tour del Mundo*. It's the first all-Spanish album to reach number one on the *Billboard* 200 chart.

2021
Bad Bunny takes part in and wins the WWE 24/7 Championship.

2022
Un Verano Sin Ti is the first Spanish-language album to be nominated for Album of the Year at the Grammys.

2025
Bad Bunny performs 31 shows in Puerto Rico, bringing more than $175 million to the island.

2026
Bad Bunny wins the Grammy for Album of the Year with the first Spanish-language album to win the prize. He then performs at the Super Bowl.

In just 10 years, Bad Bunny rose from a grocery store worker to the winner of the Album of the Year Grammy!

BAD BUNNY OFF THE STAGE

Bad Bunny has interests outside music. He loves pro **wrestling** and has taken part in WWE events. He also co-owns a Puerto Rican basketball team in San Juan called Cangrejeros de Santurce. He's also interested in different kinds of fashion and uses his style to inspire others to be themselves.

Bad Bunny started the Good Bunny Foundation in 2018. This group helps young Puerto Ricans in need through sports, music, and the arts. Bad Bunny plans to keep making a difference in Puerto Rico and around the world.

In His Words

"I am Puerto Rican, I am Caribbean, and my music, my culture, my country's history run through my veins...I want to show the world who I am, who BENITO ANTONIO is, and who PUERTO RICO is."

— Album press release from January 5, 2025

Be Like Bad Bunny!

Read more about Puerto Rico and the challenges the people there face.

Get involved in activities to help your community. Look for clean ups, events to help those in need, or public gatherings about issues you care about.

Get to know people who are different from you and speak up for them when needed.

Listen to different genres of music, including those in different languages.

Find out more about your cultural background. Think of ways you can honor it, and respect the ways other people honor their backgrounds too.

You don't need to be a superstar to be like Bad Bunny. Here are some ways to follow in his footsteps.

GLOSSARY

barrier: Something that stops movement or success.

COVID-19 pandemic: An event that began in China in 2019 in which a disease that causes breathing problems, a fever, and other health issues spread rapidly around the world and made millions of people sick in a short period of time.

culture: The beliefs and ways of life of a group of people.

dedicate: To publicly say something is made or done to honor someone.

Latino: Having to do with people from Latin America, including Puerto Rico.

LGBTQ+: Relating to a group made up of people who see themselves as a gender different from the sex they were assigned at birth or who want to be in romantic relationships that aren't only male-female. LGBTQ stands for lesbian, gay, bisexual, transgender, and queer.

nominate: To suggest someone for an honor.

protest: An event in which people gather to show they do not like something.

stereotype: An often unfair and untrue belief people have about all members of a certain group.

stream: To send music or videos through the internet so a person can play them right away.

violence: The use of force to harm someone.

wrestling: Fighting by gripping, holding, and pushing rather than hitting.

FOR MORE INFORMATION

WEBSITES

Artist: Bad Bunny

www.grammy.com/artists/bad-bunny/243129

Track Bad Bunny's nominations and wins on the Grammy Awards website.

Bad Bunny

kids.britannica.com/students/article/Bad-Bunny/633473

Read more about Bad Bunny's life on Britannica Kids.

BOOKS

Birdoff, Ariel Factor. *Bad Bunny*. Minneapolis, MN: Bellwether Media, 2025.

Earley, Christina. *Puerto Rico*. St. Catharines, ON: Crabtree Publishing, 2024.

Edelman, Claudia Romo, and Ann Dávila Cardinal. *Bad Bunny*. New York, NY: Roaring Brook Press, 2024.

INDEX